Her Whispers Within-A Poetic Odyssey of Girlhood

Amrita Sewani

BookLeaf Publishing

India | USA | UK

Presentation by *BookLeaf Publishing*

Web: www.bookleafpub.com

E-mail: info@bookleafpub.com

ISBN: 9789363316454

First edition 2024

<u>Part -I</u>

<u>IN HER OWN WORDS: SHE
WHISPERS, SHE HEARS</u>

From Rejection to Acceptance

I came into this world and opened my eyes,
with a hope to live a life as I like.
The family haunted me saying a girl had been born,
she is not the one we ever want.

They finally accepted me after feeling guilty twice,
I thought they were not bad, but wise.
They came home with a newborn in their arms,
that moment was bliss beyond any charm.

I attracted everyone who was around,
the family is still incomplete, people said in a
low sound.
This cute little girl has taken all the attention,
but something is missing from their perception.

I was little, rolling and crawling everywhere,
preparing myself to run with loads of dreams
anywhere.
The whole family helped me take my first step,
assuring I cannot walk alone and will always be
protected by them.

First Day Fears

Watching me as a 3-year-old, my parents were astounded,
with tons of new responsibilities, they would soon be surrounded.
Something seemed wrong and their worries compounded,
thinking of my first school day, they were confounded.

I woke up the next morning, with excitement so bright,
the thought of making new friends filled me with delight.
I was ready to leave with an eagerness to explore,
tears filled my eyes as I stepped out the door.

My father dropped me to school with a smile on his face,
his face,

"I will be back soon," he said in solace.
My heart was shattered as he waved his hand in
pain,
I wished this day would never come again.

I promised myself not to leave my parents from
tomorrow,
upon returning home, their smiling faces eased
my sorrow.
I was heartbroken when I heard my parents
saying,
"Our daughter will leave us forever one day,
what will we be doing?"

Childhood Confusions

It has been a few years since I started going to
school,
this routine now felt very cool.
I learned to stay at a distance from my family,
and seeing them off every day became a habit
quickly.

When started playing with friends in the park,
I had to return soon before it got dark.
Wanted to roam like my brothers, so free,
but the choices of elders always governed me.

A desire to live differently seemed complicated,
I was too young for such a topic to be debated.
Whenever I insisted on going out and playing,
I was told, "Home is where you should be
staying."

I wondered about the hidden reason,
being a child or a girl, what was the concern?
I stopped asking questions and followed their
voices,
it was the moment I felt my crisis.

Chores and Choices

In a quick splurge of time, my childhood was
gone,
not much ahead, just twelve years old at dawn.
Is it right to say I am a mature girl now,
who must handle her duties anyhow?

In my studies, I was doing great,
but was that enough as my master trait?
I was told to learn some house chores,
a girl, they said, needs this, of course.

Somehow it was manageable, perhaps not,
I knew it was not something to be taught.
My parents saw it as a misconception,
their daughter did not need such a perception.

I was happy they stood by my side,
their love and support were my constant guide.
It pinched the eyes of those nearby,
who said, "A girl shouldn't aim for the sky."

A Major Mystery

A random day in school turned terrible all of a
sudden,
it was a mystery to me, I felt like I was stricken.
Waiting for the next class after the bell to be
started,
a classmate called me, and I was startled.

I was told about something unusual,
which I'd never heard before, but it felt factual.
Everyone around consoled me and said,
"It happens to every girl; you are among the
rest."

It was a relief to hear that I was not unique,
my mind struck and questions began to peak.
When handed a napkin to apply,
I remembered the same thing at a shop nearby.

When I saw it for the first time, I tried to ask and inquired,
"You'll know in time," everyone conspired.
It is called the menstrual cycle, key to reproduction's success,
why are girls hesitant to say it is just a biological process?

The Teenage Turmoil

Teenage is the best phase of childhood,
but the experiences are not always good.
There is a constant war between inside and out,
what a teenager thinks is right without any
doubt.

Girls are extra protected as a matter of respect,
expected to be wise in every aspect.
Respect is something to earn and achieve,
girls are taught it as a status to conceive.

Whether hanging out or trying a makeover,
people criticized it as if it were a hangover.
Beauty products were tempting and flaunting,
but bringing them home felt much more
daunting.

I struggled between simplicity and attraction,
all I desired was a bit of attention.
Girls seeking attention are not liked by society,
it is viewed as a sign of unwanted curiosity.

The Struggles of a Kind Heart

Good at academics but poor in sports,
I knew my expertise lay in reports.
I was happy to excel among the many,
my parents were proud, and their joy was plenty.

My personality was calm and kind,
I could not accept being unrefined.
Having friends in school and neighbors was a
boon,
some of them were temporary, I realized that
soon.

I was loyal when it came to friendship
but struggled with deep companionship.
When I felt someone was pretending,
I would quickly distance myself, no matter the
ending.

Some said girls are arrogant, some said there are
exceptions,
I started getting judged by people's perceptions.
It was strange to see reactions from different
directions,
I thought, let it be, no need for corrections.

A Girl's Mantra

We always need to look classy,
or else, they will call us messy.
How we should look is dictated by others,
and we are immature if it does not bother us.

I wondered why this happens only with girls,
when personal choice should rule their worlds.
I felt it was wrong and wanted to bring a change,
it was not just a mindset, but a challenging race.

I asked my parents for their opinion,
curious to know, are we a union?
They held my hand and replied instantly,
"You are a princess, shout it proudly."

Yes, a princess, sounds extraordinary,
a girl is much more than just ordinary.
"I am beautiful in my way," became my mantra,
was happy not to be part of any gender drama.

Behind the Crown

The word "Princess" sounded quite weird,
to those who knew she just got pampered.
People defined a "Princess" as a lazy dictator,
who gives orders without regard for her
caretaker.

Soon, people exclaimed the word was justified,
since she always stands behind a Prince and is
'unidentified.'
I believe a Prince leads not to complete her
identity,
but to seek validation that preserves his own
dignity.

I heard everyone talking about the cultural norm,
and how I am not growing up in a proper form.

"If treated like this, how will she be carried?
Will she be a princess after getting married?"

I was stunned by this definition,
a beautiful word turned into a negative
connotation.
Once again, a gender trauma had arisen,
and dealing with this became my mind's prison.

Tied Up in Chains

A boundary was set, not meant to be crossed,
stepping out, they said, would be my loss.
A stereotype of a "good girl" became the trend,
staying within limits was the only end.

Setting limits does not make a girl strong,
it makes her weak, and that is just wrong.
Boys were free to come home on their own time,
while I was taught to be disciplined, to toe the
line.

News headlines blared across every media
station,
eve teasing and rape cases sparked a sensation.
An atmosphere of fear was constantly shown,

warning echoes for those girls walking out
alone.

Hearing those cases, every family grew wary,
more rules were imposed, stricter and scary.
The voice within me raged, asking a question,
what lies ahead for a girl, any prediction?

A Mother's Wisdom

It hit me hard when I came to know,
every girl faces this and becomes a pro.
Pro, not in accepting these myths of tradition,
but in fighting for themselves, making it a
mission.

Who will bring this change? I was completely
unsure,
the girl who is suffering or one who's endured?
The answer I found was in action,
change is coming from a girl, now in position.

Position is not just about a workplace space,
it is about being responsible in every phase.

My mother stood up against this gender-based
role,
and helped me understand my true, inner soul.

She said, "You should not be my shadow in this
case,
where being a girl is a burden, not a grace."
I felt blessed to have a mother like her,
she became my constant shield, always there.

Freedom in Tradition

Expected to learn how to behave and talk with others,
girls should be taught basic manners by their mothers.
If anything goes wrong, the blame falls strong,
on mothers who "failed" in their duties lifelong.

The rules needed to be followed in a way familiar,
not obeying them was considered a big failure.
Talking, eating, laughing, wearing—all controlled,
I was told to care for small things, burdened with a load.

I wondered why girls needed to face these
demands,
when boys were free to follow their plans.
I was annoyed with those who set these
regulations,
should I follow or ignore these conventions?

My parents said "Not all standards need
criticism,
they simply require your thoughtful wisdom."
I decided to find a loophole in each rule,
to learn and grow, not just follow like a fool.

Education Bias

At eighteen, I stopped seeking a guide,
facing life's challenges on my own, I would not
hide.
I learned to manage traditions with my voice,
and found strength and freedom in my own
choice.

After completing school, I chose to study
further,
asked what I would do if this career I prefer.
The habit of criticizing a girl has never ceased,
"Her education is not worth it," they all believed.

"Education for a girl is optional," people made a
claim,
there is no need for her recognition or fame.
"Better to save money for her marriage," they
said,

"Let go of this idea and make a wise decision
instead."

My father said, "Educating her is my pride,
I want nothing in return; let me decide.
Education is not just for future delights,
it will help her stand strong for her rights."

Echoes of Past

Being my strength, my father once said,
"You have a good heart, that's your strength.
You may face small struggles at every stage,
But your achievements will roar and engage."

He used to praise me in front of everyone,
"She always makes me proud," he'd say to
anyone.
One day he left his wife and children forever,
and his words echo as a memory that ends never.

It felt like a responsibility came up so early,
"How will we survive?" was my question,
surely.
Each day reminded me of the need for money,
"Let's do something," so Mom would not worry.

I started working, though the pay was small,
people said it was not a big call.
It was the choice of a 19-year-old girl,
to learn how to survive in this world's swirl.

Self-Worth

Some called it pressure, some called it
compromise,
and different opinions flew, but I aimed to rise.
My family tree stood strong, always by my side,
their constant support kept my spirit alive.

There were times when I felt so low,
lost in what I was doing and unsure where to go.
Chasing dreams cannot always be in full stride,
putting family first is a challenge, and not
everyone can abide.

At twenty-one, gender trauma again reflected,
"Time to marry," they said, "She is now
graduated."
Once again, my dreams felt suffocated,

for a girl, why must everything be
time-allocated?

I then pursued higher education, not for fame,
there was a need to change this gender game.
But around me, I heard some opinions taking a
twist,
after marriage, "there may be no career on your
list."

Being Unstoppable

Education is meant to broaden your mind's
scope,
to navigate challenges with wisdom and hope.
I decided to go ahead with this mindset,
knowledge never goes to waste; I was fully set.

Mastering my course, doubts I did reject,
now a girl earned respect and no longer neglect.
An opinionated, strong girl set her goal in sight,
I stood tall and proud, shining in my own light.

Being born a girl, is worth every bit,
with supporters saying, "You can do it!"
None of this was possible without my family's
backing,
through every obstacle, beside me, they were
tracking.

I was amazed by my strength in this situation,
I chose my partner; marriage was now "my"
decision.
They say achievements secure you financially,
but some victories cannot be measured
monetarily.

Myths of Marriage

Gender myths whispered close to my ear,
"Marriage is tough for women," I would hear.
I knew this was true for many all along,
here is the story of married women, capable and
strong.

"It will not be easy to maintain the same glow,
as before marriage when you used to flow.
More responsibilities will fill your routine,
not every dream can be pursued, no matter how
keen.

If you go out to work and earn,
you will soon make others discern.
You will be told to follow the guide,
your decisions get ignored and pushed aside."

I wondered how to cope if this was my fate too,
how I'd be judged, I had no clue.
Passing through girlhood was no easy feat,
entering womanhood is tougher and deep.

A Happy Mission

I have entered a new phase of life,
in another family, aiming to shine bright.
Duties and expectations would be high,
but my story was different—I let out a sigh.

My new family welcomed me with open arms,
helping me adjust and keep away from harm.
Outsiders called it modern foolishness,
saying, "She is just your son's wife, nothing
more or less."

I was treated in a way they did not expect,
my opinions were heard, and no rules were set.
I was free to decide and carry my vision,
marriage is bliss when it is a happy mission.

Nothing is hard with amazing compatibility,
my husband and his family are perfect in every
reality.
Getting love and respect beyond what I
expected,
blessed once more, with such souls I am
connected.

I Own My Choices

Whether deemed foolish or selfish, it is true,
it depends if I follow society's view.
I never mind this kind of noise,
selfish or foolish, let it be my choice.

People may say I lack logic's knack,
but I know when to step back on track.
Whether seen as sentimental or practical,
I proudly embody both; that is factual.

When I stand up to wrongs, I break a norm
that is fine, I am ready to face the storm.
I own my choices and their weight,
yet people worry, it is their trait.

Strength comes from facing big challenges,
but I find strength in life's balances.

My life is balanced with love and
responsibilities,
seeing dreams with ease and abilities.

Let's Celebrate Ourselves

Some days a happy soul, some days a broken
heart,
most days, we are both, and still surpass.
Standing tall, fighting, and changing the scene,
we know how to act in different forms on screen.

Our looks, clothes, and habits define our
identity,
people judge quickly in this era of "modernity."
It is all in the mindset, we combine all traits,
we are remarkable, no matter any judgments
they create.

Whether we work or stay at home,
we are nurturers, that is well-known.
Feminism is not about being like men,
we are simply different, embrace that again.

No one sees the internal battles we have fought,
what we endured is a matter of thought.
Let us celebrate how we made it shine,
we are proud of ourselves, that is truly divine.

Part-II

She is BLOSSOMING now

Part I captures the moments when she whispered to herself about how she wanted to shape her life.

Part II reveals the transformations that followed those whispers. She emerges as a new person, standing strong and ready to face the challenges of womanhood.

Dancing with Freedom

An independent girl is seen as careless,
but she is capable and full of awareness.
Independence is not selfish, it is true,
it is a graceful art where she plays her part too.

She balances her freedom with love and care,
having choices and leading a life fair.
She finds her rhythm, strong and free,
dancing with independence for all to see.

Curiosity fills her with light,
exploring the world and seeking what is right.
Many questions flow and ideas bloom,
in her mind, there is always an empty room.

Wondering, learning, growing each day,
proudly forging her way.
She navigates her paths with new views,
she is special because she is a girl with clues.

The Art of Self-Healing

Crying might seem like a weak emotion,
but it heals, no matter the situation.
It is not a weakness to hide,
but a strength that shows what is inside.

A girl lets her feelings flow,
a brave act that helps her grow.
Her strength is unseen yet deeply felt,
a powerful force that guides her to act.

She seeks support as her personal choice,
nothing to do with gender, just her voice.
With time and patience, she has found,
peace and wholeness all around.

This path of healing a girl must tread,
mending wounds and moving ahead.
Through trials and pain, healing takes place,
restoring her spirit, she finds grace.

One-Sided Forgiveness

It is good to let go and clear the mental space,
though sometimes it is a challenge to face.
A girl hides her wounds with care,
her journey of forgiveness is everywhere.

She wonders why it is expected of her,
to forgive so easily, especially as a girl.
Whether playing as a child or out on the street,
if something goes wrong, she is told to retreat.

Everyone seeks peace and release,
but she cannot express it with ease.
If she shows her feelings and anger,
she is called dramatic, just an "imager."

"Let go and move on," they always say,
but why should it only be her way?
It is an art, but they have made it gender-based,
anyway, she is more peaceful in this case.

Silence is Power

Silence is seen as the greatest praise,
when talking about a girl's ways.
She is not allowed to speak much at all,
it is seen as a flaw, if she dares stand tall.

When she speaks or laughs out loud,
people say it is unnecessary, and not allowed.
They think she lacks manners, it is so,
if she is loud, she is making a mess, oh!

One day, deep in thought, it became clear,
silence is power, not something to fear.
Though her personality is shy and restrained,
but it is never too late to accept and change.

Speaking is not bad, but ignoring is,
she must speak up to keep her boundaries in
bliss.

She still has moments of silence and space,
where she finds her peace and chase.

Courage in the Fears

The voice of fear, nobody wants to hear,
yet it shadows a girl, always near.
Whenever she stands brave in front of it,
people say she has no shame and spirit.

It is not true she lacks fear inside,
but she stands strong, reversing the tide.
She faces challenges by standing tall,
and is never afraid to give her all.

With courage as her guiding star,
she knows when to step ahead, near or far.
Sometimes she steps back, not from defeat,
she is just waiting for her moment to speak.

She confronts her fears, no matter the distance,
her every move is a star of persistence.
Proving her strength with each new test,
with every challenge, her courage is at its best.

Mastering the Balance

51

Everyone juggles between dreams and real life,
but a girl knows how to balance both with no
strife.
Her heart is full of dreams, her mind so wise,
that she chases her goals and reaches for the
skies.

She makes compromises, but her dreams stay fit,
finds her path with no chance to undo it.
She navigates life with a vision so clear,
a challenge to those who fear her cheer.

When a boy wins, it is a source of pride,
but when a girl wins, they question her stride.
If she chooses her path, they call her stubborn,
but they forget, nobody owns another's burden.

She has got skills that truly shine,
balancing dreams and reality, all in line.
Managing work and home, she is on the go,
making it all work, she is a real pro.

Path to Self-Love

Self-love is a journey, not easily taught,
to love yourself is the best lesson sought.
A girl is told to please everyone around,
but through trials and doubts, her path is found.

She is told to love others first,
putting herself last, it seems a curse.
Her needs are hidden, her desires set aside,
her wishes and dreams often pushed to hide.

She gets used to putting herself last,
depending on others' feelings and holding fast.
She cares for her family, even when she is ill,
and strange when no one steps up to help her
still.

She knows her worth with time's embrace,
and happy with herself, she lights up the place.
With self-love, she faces her fears,
gaining confidence through the years.

Shattering Stereotypes

Various stereotypes set for a girl,
meant to define her in this world.
If she dares to break even one,
her journey becomes a matter of fun.

"Daughter of a respected family" is a common
role,
obvious to obey, with a heavy toll.
She is not supposed to raise her voice,
if she does, they question her choice.

It hits hard when she breaks any mold,
becoming more than the story told.
When she defies the roles set by society,
she redefines norms with her variety.

Though she is told what she should or should not
be,
she moves ahead and becomes bold and free.
With each step, she shatters the norms,
telling a tale that is yet to transform.

The Beauty of Resilience

Resilience is a powerful wave in a girl's life,
calming her through every storm and strife.
The world thinks she is scared of the fight,
but she faces it with all her might.

Stubborn when it comes to her self-respect,
no one has the right to disrespect.
If she is silent through any mean behavior,
her resilience grows even stronger.

No matter how tough it seems,
she surpasses with ease, pursuing her dreams.
She bounces back from every fall,
and remains brave through it all.

Each setback sets up her comeback,
her spirit is a flashback.
Her power shines in every role,
doubt it? History tells it all.

Her Intuition Speaks

Intuition is her inner coach,
a quiet voice that guides her approach.
She trusts her heart and instincts true,
knowing they are important, too.
.

When she feels something's not quite right,
her intuition urges her to hold tight.
She feels the thoughts you try to hide,
she knows how hard you pretend inside.

They say a girl hides emotions in her heart,
for that is where answers truly start.
No further clarity she needs to seek,
her inner voice tells when you intend to cheat.

Her intuition leads her to new experiences,
in all big and small decisions.
She is the strongest with this inner wisdom,
she is the creator of her kingdom.

Empowering Others

Empowering others is a rare delight,
a strategy not used by many in sight.
When a girl empowers, it is a gift she gives,
in her care, everyone freely lives.

It is a quality she proudly bears,
lifting others with her loving cares.
She nurtures dreams and fuels the goals,
helping everyone find their roles.

Well, let me tell you society's view,
empowered girls face harsh reviews.
They say they break the female unity,
and claim they lack the needed sensitivity.

Rejection comes from all around,
but her strength must be renowned.
It is a trait from which she is not feared,
as she brings change that will be cheered.

Thankful Heart

Gratitude is a girl's daily song,
she does not dwell on what has gone wrong.
Counting blessings with each new day,
she finds joy in this simple play.

Happiness means something unique for each,
for her, it is acceptance within her reach.
Life would not always be perfect or right,
she now knows to avoid the blame and fight.

Each day is beautiful and full of life,
she appreciates it even if it has a negative side.
Plans may not unfold as she thought,
but the future shows it is what she sought.

With a grateful heart, she faces every emotion,
she is a fighter with a belief in her devotion.
Her gratitude brings joy and peace,
turning dilemmas and worries into ease.

Choosing Healthy Relations

Sensitivity is a girl's superpower,
in it, she blooms in a love shower.
She fulfills her duties in every relation,
seeing who is real and who is just an imitation.

Always giving her all in every tie,
yet seldom receives even a single reply.
They want her to expect nothing in return,
being sensitive and patient, always waiting her
turn.

She is often rejected by society's part,
when she chooses not to give from her whole
heart.
Choosing her limits is not a crime,
to be first, stop calling her "secondary" all the
time.

Now she chooses her relations wisely,
no more fake and toxic ties, concisely.
She needs no praise, no validation turns,
she chooses who deserves her concerns.

Her Priorities Are Everything

Life flows smoothly when priorities are set,
clarity in chaos is the best you can get.
For a girl, priorities are often seen as a fuss,
in a family's eyes, she must not discuss.

Taking a stand and going slow,
to things against her values, she says no.
But if she sets her priorities straight,
she lacks emotion and cannot relate.

With limited choices, she is labeled unkind,
accused of being rigid, she lacks a flexible mind.
She is not a people pleaser anymore,
she knows who values her for sure.

Her priorities are now crucial and strong,
and the burden of pleasing reduces where she
does not belong.
Devoted to her sorted list, clear and true,
whether family, work or what she chooses to do.

Celebrating Small Victories

Victories are often seen as big and grand,
milestones that feed our desires in hand.
True happiness sparkles in small halt,
often ignored and not given much thought.

A girl sees success in the little things,
in moments others dismiss or ignore their rings.
To her, these tiny wins are the odds,
as with each small victory, her new story
unfolds.

From family's acceptance free of bias's sway,
to finishing her studies and landing a job on her
way.
Finding true love and a child to hold tight,
these small victories bring her pure delight.

She faces criticism with each goal to achieve,
so, she treasures small joys that bring her heart
relief.
Though some may view a small win as not a big
deal,
it is her way of showing just how she feels.

She is Bringing a Change

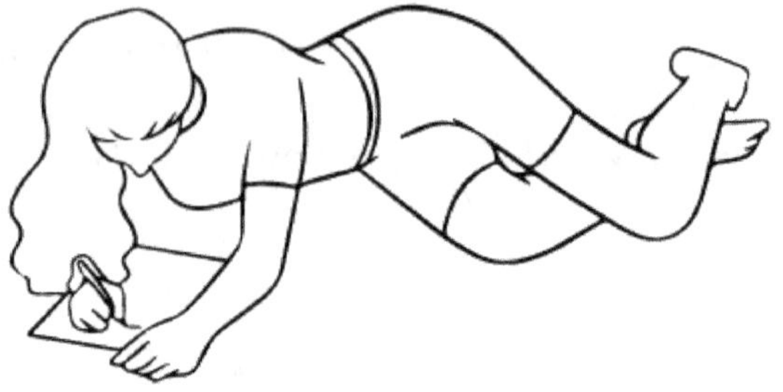

Adopting change takes effort and time,
especially when a girl starts to climb.
She brings hope and seeks to evolve,
but the world pushes her to dissolve.

Change is disliked when it is her idea,
they put her down and reject the criteria.
They call her selfish and seeking fame,
when she shows change, they destroy her name.

She is a game changer when she is resolute,
her struggles shine when she reaches the
absolute.
To some, her success is a plan to uproot,
but do not miss to see the battles she has gone
through.

Now she has no fear of criticism's weight,
she believes in herself and her passion's fate.

With loved ones by her side in every quest,
she credits them when she achieves her best.

67

Thriving in Solitude

Since birth, a girl is taught to never be alone,
at home or out, always a companion shown.
First with parents, then with a family to call,
the world feels harsh when she stands tall.

She grows used to people always around,
fearful of solitude, her heart feels bound.
She is dependent on others for her every need,
believing she is weak, alone she cannot lead.

She is told to step aside when she asks for
anything,
but must give her best if they want something.
Now she learns solitude is the best skill to save,
from which she is no longer bound to behave.

Solitude does not mean she is living in
ignorance,

it simply means she is free from peace's
hindrance.
More joyful, peaceful, and living free,
doing all the things she is meant to be.

Stronger as One

In a world that often ignores her viability,
a girl struggles to find support from her
community.
She is fighting with each other, it is known,
not seeing another girl's battle as her own.

She is beautiful in her ways,
yet the world compares her in many ways.
She deserves equality, no matter her track,
in marks, career, looks, or style, she does not
lack.

But through highs and lows, she now stands as
one,
constantly shining in the long run.
Solidarity is a powerful force she is acting for,
the world is now watching her at the core.

Always lifting each other when someone falls,
she wipes the tears but never drops her calls.
Sharing her fears and goals with her other self,
in this support, together she finds her wealth.

Passing Down Strength

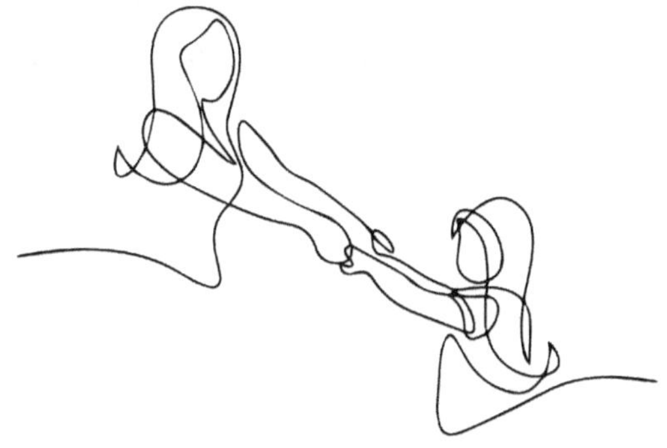

As time passes, their voices remain,
girls who fought, their battles sustain.
From the past to the present, their strength
endures,
passing knowledge to others with lessons so
pure.

From grandmothers' tales to mothers' advice,
she moves with courage and creates legacies
twice.
As a female mentor, she set an example so fine,
the race is never-ending as her courage is divine.

She shares her secrets with the next in line,
lifting their courage and helping them shine.
Living with young hearts to play her part,
and creating a better version of herself, that is
her art.

Every girl around her is a role model,
helping her find her way through the muddle.
With every word and action, she teaches a deed,
planting seeds of strength that we all need.

Unapologetically Embracing Herself

By fulfilling roles and responsibilities,
she forgets her capabilities.
Striving to be perfect in all life hacks,
there is always something in which she lacks.

Then comes a time when she sees,
she makes others happy by fitting societal needs.
At this moment she starts to embrace,
her individuality becomes her golden grace.

She sees her worth and sets the stage,
writing a story on her page.
In a world that tries to defame,
she proudly shines making her name.

Whether it is me or it is you,
girls need to support each other too.

Perfect feminism will light up the world,
when she embraces every girl making flags
unfurled.

ACKNOWLEDGEMENT

I want to thank my husband, Lavesh, for inspiring my passion for writing. His guidance was invaluable in writing this book and his understanding of a girl's journey in life is beyond words. I never imagined I could be called an author one day. Without his motivation, I might have given up on the idea of turning my writing into a published book.

I sincerely thank my brother, Ravi, for consistently motivating me and instilling a love for reading books. Seeing such men in my life supporting and inspiring me through all phases is truly heartening. I extend my deepest gratitude to my parents and in-laws for encouraging and believing in me in every endeavor I undertake.

I am grateful to those who have given me opportunities and guided me as mentors throughout my career. Whether as a hiring manager, senior, or colleague, I have been fortunate to work with great people who have enriched my workplace experiences.

I would like to thank every girl in society who has inspired me in countless ways to write this book. Although I am the author of this book, it is written on behalf of every girl who has a similar story in some way. Most of the whispers I mentioned in this book are my own experiences too.

I extend my heartfelt thanks to my Publishing Consultant, Shivani, who transformed my writing into a published reality. Her support at every stage of the publication process has helped the book reach readers in corners of the world I could not have reached alone.

I want to thank the editor, Ritika Dubey, for her feedback on the book's content. Her suggestions have allowed me to maintain the book's originality, of which I am proud. I would also like to thank the designer, Mujtaba Feroz Shah, for designing an amazing book cover that resonates with the audience and helps them understand what the book is all about.

Behind every successful author lies the unwavering support from the audience. I sincerely thank the readers for investing their valuable time in reading this book.